DOGS I HAVE KISSED

TRISTA MATEER

Editing by Clementine von Radics
www.clementinepoetry.com

Cover & Interior Art by Krystle Alder
www.krystlealder.com

for S.—

I read somewhere that dedications are like coded love letters,
but I always seem to lay us out bare.

Sorry for the poems.

Contents

BITE

I Am a Runner

I have been told that girls always fall
for men like their fathers,
but I found it a hard concept to grasp
when he was always gone
and I grew up on radio static
and blackberry preserves.

I remember having smaller hands
and looking at him through wider eyes
like everything
was so much grander
just because it was so much bigger than me
and he was so much bigger than me
so he must be grand too;
for a long time, I thought that he was,
but now words like *sweetheart* and *princess*
make me straighten my back
and shuffle my feet: back and forth, back and forth
always on the move.

I am a runner (just like my father)
only we prefer leaving
to lacing up sneakers and hitting the track.

The first boy I loved used to start our mornings
kissing my forehead in the high school lobby—
until one of his friends laughed and said:
"What are you? Her father?"
and I realized why I liked his careless mouth
so much.

I used to bury my face in his clothes
because I liked the smell:
cheap beer, cigarettes, Old Spice cologne.
And I knew it from somewhere,
I knew it from somewhere,
I knew it from

the way my father used to lean in
and smooth back my hair,
plant a kiss on my forehead
before he left for work.

Sometimes the noises of mouths still make me upset:
kissing, chewing, breathing, slurring speech.
Shouting makes my insides jump up my throat.

Once my mother said to me,
she said: "You're going to fall for men
like your father; I'm sorry—"

and I wanted to ask her if that meant
I would fall for a fighter
and a hard fist and a fast car,
boys on motorcycles,
people who ran from their problems,
midnight phone calls from the beds of other women,
slippery mouths with tongues that twisted truth
like cherry stems

or if that meant I might just be comfortable
with absence.

For the One Who Loved My Hands
More than Anything Else

You saw only what you wanted to.
There were flowers blooming between my teeth,
promises wrapped around my hips,
handstands in the gangly corners of me.

There were blades in my hands.
I was carving my name into your side
and you were calling me soft,
calling me gentle.

I do not think you were paying attention.

Texts I Shouldn't Have Sent to My Ex:

can we say goodbye again? i miss the way you rip me open.

i know your mother never liked me. i hope she knows we drank her wine and fucked on the living room couch. i bet she's where you got your stubborn mouth from.

you were supposed to write me a song for my eighteenth birthday and you never did; do you remember that? i remember that. i don't know why, but it's the first thing i tell people when you come up in conversation.

sometimes i think i resented you so much it felt like love.

you're the only person i didn't mind sleeping next to. i could never fall asleep next to the one after you. i still can't sleep.

i saw a photo of you holding a baby this morning. it fucked up my entire day. thanks.

i hate that i never hated you. i tried really hard for a long time.

do you still love me?

every time i delete your number from my phone, i write it down somewhere because i have no self control. sometimes i miss you and i don't mean to.

hey, me again.

How to Not Forgive

When I was small, I remember my mother saying that she
believed aliens helped build the pyramids. She used to keep
crystals around. She used to carry healing stones. She used to
believe my father would always come back to her.

Now that she is older, she prays to the nail marks in
someone's palms but I don't think she believes in forgiveness
anymore. She sent me to Sunday school in little floral
dresses, not to torture me but to learn this.

Hurt me once: shame on me. Hurt me twice: shame on me.
Hurt me three times: shame on me but fuck you. Hurt me four
times and we'll get severed-head biblical. We will pick up
stones.

And now that I am older, I don't give a damn about sin.
I will be the first to cast one.

I Was Nineteen Years Old

When I found out that you could cry
"please no, please don't, please no, please don't"
loud enough to wake the neighbors
and they still wouldn't turn on a porch light.

And I never wanted to tell anyone
but the poems

because I was the one with the pink garter belt
and the thigh-high stockings. And I was the one
with the little black dress.

I was the one
who still tried to kiss him afterward
because I thought that might
make it okay.

It didn't.

The Poem That Begged Not to Be Written

For the one who broke me like bread
at the dining table and then left mid-meal.

For the one who called himself an animal
so I didn't have to.

For the one who cut me in half and scooped out
all of my nice, all of my forgiving, all of my trust.

For the one who cheated
and for the one who bruised
and for the one who left.

I learned the word *fuck* from my mother's tongue,
as in *fucker, he fucking left me,
he fucking left.*

I learned the word *no* from myself.
From somewhere deep in the pit of me,
it rose like some ancient thing
and slunk its way out of my throat,
heavy-handed.

Will I ever let this guard down long enough
to learn anything new?

Fuck no.

When I Was a Little Girl

In the bone-white basement of a church, a woman
told me that I was made from the rib of a man.

I tried to count my brother's ribs because I wanted
to ask why he had the same number as me and
shouldn't he have one less? Or maybe two less,
depending on how many little girls God wanted to
make when my brother was born?

Instead I asked, if I were a little rib girl,
then what was my brother made of?

She told me that man was created from dust and
breath in the image of God; and I tried to imagine
that God looked like my brother when he lost his
two front teeth in a bicycle accident and ran
screaming into the house, crying for my mother
with his bloody mouth.

I asked why God couldn't be more like Mom instead.
And she said to me, "women are sinful."

Years later when I taste my first one, I agree with her.

This Is How New Religions Start

Waking up too early because your breath
is heavy
in the bed next to me:
wide-eyed-awake early morning reveries.

I could probably make a sermon
out of the way your mother looks at me.

I could probably make a sermon
out of the way you mouth words in your sleep.

Light slipping through the curtains,
every part of you looks saccharine.

I want to wash your feet with my hair.
I want to rinse my mouth out with soap.
I want to wash your feet with my hair.
I want to rinse my mouth out with soap.

Violets, Violets, Violets

Girl like a flower that bloomed only at night,
I spent months unfurling by your bedside.
In the beginning
the empty wine bottles on the bathroom floor
seemed flirty, somehow mysterious.
But when the sun came up, I looked stark by contrast.
Everything looked bright, so bright
laid out next to the bags under my eyes.
Violets, violets, violets.

And you with your lungfuls of hope,
teeth like slick wet promises
every time you opened your mouth.
We used to do so much talking
before things got quiet here.
We used to do so much not-talking.
You with your doe eyes, you with those lips
that could almost suck stubbornness out of anybody.
You with your wishful thinking.
You with that hope.

After a while you started to resent the color purple,
the way my apologies
surfaced like bruises after the fact.

After a while it was those violets, violets, violets.
Girl like a garden you never volunteered to tend.
Dirt all tracked into your front hall.

Picking New Sheets

When I replace these, there's no
going back.

When I throw these out,
the only thing that will remember
your small ragged-breath sleeping
will be me.

No more touch memory on my pillowcases.
No more "I can almost smell you."

I think the walls
of this room have already forgotten
you used to breathe here.

For Brittanie

There will always be men
who have fishhooks for fingers.
There will always be women
with wet, sharp mouths.
It is okay to get caught up in them.

It is not okay to drown.

Don't you ever let another human
being tear you apart.
Remember that you have claws
and teeth, too.

Remember that you are better off

whole.

Apartment #9

I am not going to miss you.
You are not going to miss me:
the filler conversation in your empty bed.

I know we both said some nice things in the end
but I already forget the shape of your mouth
and the night you cradled my face in your hands
and said, "You're so pretty, you're so pretty"—

almost, anyway. But I swear

in a week, I will not remember how
I moaned for your hands
or spent an hour on public transit
just to get to your front door
with a careless grin and smudged lipstick;

in a month, I will not remember anything.

Not even the scent of your skin
after a whole day in bed
with me.

Not even the way we said goodbye.

Barbed Wire

Boys are always trying to fix me:
taking me home like a weekend project,
all pursed lips and furrowed brows
when I don't snap out of it with a kiss.

Approach me like I weave caution tape into my hair.

I will greet you with a mouth full of barbed wire
until you learn to stop coming after me
with your hands.

4/23

I don't know how to exist properly
in the same space as someone
I don't love anymore.

I Want to Be Sorry for This

I wrote our breakup poem
two weeks after we started "going steady."
I wrote our breakup poem before I ever said:
I love you. I wrote our breakup poem before
we moved in together.

My hands are still shaking from
nights spent not knowing
how to want you.

Sorry I Stole Your DVD When We Broke Up

We sat on your couch in your basement apartment
that had somehow become *our* basement apartment
with the dim lighting and the wet air.
The pages of my books curled.
My dresses smelled like mildew.

We sat on our couch in our basement apartment
for the same date night that we had every Wednesday.
With bad Chinese take-out
and a movie that you already owned,
we sat for an hour and forty-two minutes
before I ever dreamt of leaving.

We sat on our couch in our basement apartment
while the credits rolled
and you expressed your frustration with the ending;
and oceans parted inside of me with urgency.
Looking around at dirty clothes and empty bottles,
I got seasick for the first time in my life.

We sat on our couch in our basement apartment
while you ejected the movie and tucked it away
and I hung my Y's back up.

Your couch. Your basement apartment.
Your complacency.

Not mine.

Keys on the Coffee Table

I had played the string-along game.
I had done my fair share of pushing away.
I was all tease and no follow-through,
all *want me but don't depend on me.*

I was an evader of intimacy.
I sought out commitment until it came knocking.
Then I was diving out of first-story windows
and hiding in the bushes.

You were the first person I ever really ran from.
Bags packed while you were at work,
phone calls ignored.

I took off wordlessly,
effortlessly.

I planned it for weeks
and still kissed you goodnight.
It was so goddamn easy.

I thought I'd feel guilt wedged up
under my ribcage somewhere.
I thought I'd feel remorse.

But I took that first step out the door
and all I felt was

free.

You Will Teach Her to Spit Out My Name

When you fall into the arms of someone new
I will just be the mess of a woman
who left your love notes on the floor
and ran off.

When you bring up the past,
I will be the monster you could never outrun.
I will be the fear in the back of your throat
and nothing more.

I will be an unfortunate thing to overcome,
not a person with a handful of fuck-ups
and a mouthful of apologies.

The Poet
After Caitlyn Siehl

The poet can't stand the quiet. She can't stand
the buzzing in her head. The murmur of memory.
The poet picks up a book of poetry. It is not her
writing but it reads the same way. It is not her
story but the ending is similar enough to pass.
The poet tries to read a verse out loud and only
tastes blood in her mouth.

The poet worries she is writing the same poem
over and over. No matter what words she puts down,
it comes out with a bite. It says *I love you* with a
mouth full of bone.

The poet wants to stop writing about love and
predators but when she puts down the pen, she
always finds the poems anyway.

I Want to Fuck You but Your Mother's in Town

Your body is not my favorite body.
I do not know its ins and outs.
It does not feel like a safe harbor to me;
but there is familiarity in it.
It is the closest body I feel comfortable
curling up with.
It is a good body.
It stands to attention when I enter a room,
but it does not hold my interest.
I do not dwell on your body
unless I am digging around for ways to
make myself shudder and shake alone.
I do not contemplate the curve of it
over a cup of tea.
It is where I want to be sometimes,
but not where I want to end up.

Sweet Tea and Seven Other Texan Cliches

My girl
doesn't like to write
confessional poetry,

roadmaps through her becomings for strangers.
I admire the way she refuses to sell tickets to her own event,
like her life is not a spectator sport
like she doesn't need a metaphor for my mouth
(and if she has one, I'll never know what it is).

My girl
tastes like
fear of change,

tastes like spurs without the boots, without the cowboy
tastes like sweet tea and seven other Texan cliches.
She writes a lot about religion
for someone who looks out of place in a pew.
She subscribes to the bible of mouth to mouth
(and gin, and sweat).
She makes me want to ransack my own temple.

My girl
always talks about herself
like she's a graveyard,

a place for other people to come and bury what they've lost.
As much as I want to tell her that she's wrong,
I still find myself crouching in her earth
with flowers I've brought for someone else.

My girl says, "come on, baby, lay it on me"
and I still don't know if she's talking about my story

or my mouth.

RE: I Thought I Found the One

In your anger and your despair
and your glorious, glorious youth
do not discount the idea of soul mates.

Discount the idea of a singular soulmate.

You still have way too much to learn
to be taught by one person.
It's going to take a lot of time.
It's going to take a lot of long nights
and willing mouths.

And you might curse the one who teaches you
what it feels like to cry at the bottom of the shower
in the middle of the night,
but it is important to learn
how to get back up on your own feet
and let the wolf in your throat howl at the moon
once in a while.

Spit out the name of the one
who teaches you how to let go.

Keep every love note from the one who shows you
how to want yourself only when he stops calling you.
Use them like blueprints when you forget
what it sounds like to ache.

They're not all gonna be bad.
Some of them burn.

Some of them feel like sinking
into the heavy belly of the sun
and sure, sure—
You never come away from something like that
without a few burn marks

but I promise it's worth the warmth.

Remember,
every time you think you've found "the one,"
there's probably going to be just one more.

And you're still gonna love
every single damn one of them
like they were the most important sucker
on the planet.

In this life, you're going to love like pulling teeth,
(one after another)
and that's okay.

I promise it's all right.

Communist Love Poem

You taste like a 1979 Shiraz.
You taste like the Berlin Wall coming down.
You taste like a powder keg
and honey, all I want to do is set you off.

You remind me of fir trees in the winter and
fir trees in the summer,

and that sweet pang right before a headache sets in:
you know you're in for it.

I am so in for it.

I Wish There Was a Better Way to Say This:

the way you yank smiles out of me
like stubborn teeth
scares the shit out of me.

Plums

I spend too much time
thinking about fucking you;
admittedly, somehow
that seems more acceptable
than all the time I spend
thinking about
silly things
like my head on your chest
and whether or not you'd like my
mother's recipes
or my affinity for pitted fruits.

For Selene Who Is Not Dead but Wanted to Be

The first time you told me that you wanted to kill yourself, I should have called your mother instead of letting you think you could rely on something as shifty and indifferent as me. I shouldn't have written you poetry. I should have cradled the phone like a newborn and driven all the way to Texas, shown up on the doorstep in that indiscriminate heat just to open my arms to you.

It's just that I am selfish and gas is expensive and it's hard to tell the difference between wanting to die and just wanting to sink for a while. It's just that I knew a boy once who said those words to me only when he wanted my undivided attention and my legs spread in the back of his car. It's just that I thought it was one thing to want to die and another thing to pick up kitchen knives.

When you showed me that it was the same thing, I went through an entire season of not even wanting to stand near cutting boards because of the steady chop chop chop. Because of the slice. Removing the skin. Cutting out the bad bits. It's like watching someone yanking out weeds from the root when you have dandelion veins.

I had a dream a few weeks ago of throwing all the sharp objects in your house onto the roof. I had a dream about burying them in the backyard so you couldn't lay out treasure maps on your skin anymore.

I had a dream about driving all the way to Texas just to end up crying in your mother's lap.

I'm sorry it took me so long to understand. And I am sorry that I ended up understanding too well. I am still selfish and gas prices are still high and now I spend too much time having to wrap my arms around myself to ever let go long enough to hold someone else together.

I should have called your mother. I should have called your mother. I should have called your mother.

Blame the Writer in You

You meet him at the train station, twenty minutes
late. He smiles anyway.

You breathe. You breathe. You breathe.

He says, "I was nervous about our date so I looked
you up on the Internet. I saw your poetry."

You breathe. You breathe. You breathe.

He tilts his head to the side, all posturing, all posed.
Like a mannequin. Like a movie still. Like five other men
you've been on dates with this month. He asks if
you are going to write about him.

And you growl.

But you do.

"I Thought You'd Be Taller"

I'm sorry we didn't meet at a better time in my life.

I couldn't give you what you wanted
when you wanted it.
Later I tried to yank it out of you from the root,
but you had none of it.

I'm sorry that I am back and forth,
push and pull
instead of effortless simplicity.

A Brief Note on Leaving Behind
Things Not Meant for You

Caitlyn tells me that she is proud of me
for not compromising myself and I thank her.

I do not tell her that sometimes it feels like
compromising yourself is part of growing up.

I Want to Kiss Your Knees

I'm sorry.
It's 5:30 a.m. and I want
unconventional pieces of you
pressed between my lips.

Texts I Shouldn't Have Sent to My Ex (part 2):

do you need help with your okcupid profile? i'm really good at getting boring strangers interested in me.

the last time we saw each other, i told you that my mother was on her way home just because i wanted to get you out of my bed. i want to be sorry for that.

i know that it's stupid, but there are places i can't go without thinking of you and it makes me angry. subway. the pizzeria by my house. i can't use my orange sheets anymore.

you were right about my mother, by the way. i think it was the only thing you were right about.

i hate that your life is more together than mine. i was supposed to be the one going places. i was supposed to be able to look down on you. i feel like i'm still stuck on your bedroom floor with my summer dress pulled to the side.

i bought a new vibrator this year. it reminded me of dating you. i wish i'd had one then.

i loved her more than i loved you and i'm sorry that you knew it.

sometimes i wonder if we're still supposed to end up together even though i don't love you and the sound

of your voice makes me want to send my fist through a wall.

in the spirit of christmas, i think we should fuck.

do you want my new number?

Garnish with a Lime Wedge

You know that feeling when you drink too much
of a certain liquor and then even the sight of it
makes you feel unsteady?

That's how I feel when I write poems about you.

Tonight I kissed three people on the mouth
because I still don't know what you taste like.

I am always two parts tequila,
one part longing.

Peaches

You've ruined peaches for me.

I can't eat one without thinking of your hands
dipping into my soft flesh, mouth dripping,
teeth skimming across skin, tongue lapping
at the excess:

greedy, greedy, greedy.

I am all rush and blush at a summer picnic lunch,
hands shaking at the farmers' market.

The Dogs I Have Kissed

The last time I kissed a boy,
it was so dark that I could feel him out only
by the brush of his cheeks on mine,
the smoke of his cigarette mouth,
the dim glow of receding headlights.
It was a tequila kiss, a light beer brush up,
domestic names in plastic cups,
sloppy fingers and sloppier mouths;

I bit down on his bottom lip
until he pulled away
with a scowl

and I wanted it to be you.
I wanted it to be you
so bad I'd settle for less than lips.

I'd suck salt off your fingers
like a fucking animal.

SFO: Flight UA 500
Connection time: 1 hour, 35 minutes

This is the closest I have been to you in four months.

Sometimes I think I will always be stuck
writing poetry to you from airport lounges,
waiting for connecting flights
to take me somewhere I'm not sure I want to be.

Anywhere more than a breath away
from your warm morning mouth
is somewhere I'm not sure I want to be.

How many times do you think I would have blushed
at your touch in ninety-five minutes?

Headspace
For My Saint Kilda One Night Stand

Tired of fighting but still fighters, we took to your sheets
armed with skin and teeth. It has been a month since I bested
your body in bed.

I am sorry if you knew my head was somewhere else. It is so
strange to be pressed up against someone's mouth and to be,
at the same time, nearly eight thousand miles away in the
arms of a man with a softer smile and bigger hands.

You kept looking at my face and I wanted to ask if you saw
me, or if you saw only the woman who took one of your
bookshelves and most of the pictures off the walls when she
left. I am sorry that I could not fill your bare apartment. I am
glad that I could fill the void she left in your palms.

I don't know what it is in me that yearns to be the lifeboat
that people throw themselves at when they are drowning. I
wanted to taste the salt on your skin, to press my mouth
against the violent curve of you.

When we met, you recited the list of girls you'd been through
since your breakup. You didn't use any of their names. I still
wonder what my euphemism is—whether I'm the American
or the girl who wrote a poem about fucking you. Maybe I will
be both. Maybe I don't even make the list.

For me, you are the thirty-three-hour date, and the man who
takes his tea the way I take mine in the morning when no one
else is around: too much milk, too much honey. You are the
man I refused to kiss goodbye.

I could have spent a week in your bed.

To Myself: On the Plane

You kiss boys like you practiced on juice boxes,
always reaching for one last drop.
You kiss girls like you really believe
slow and steady is the way to win a race.
You don't kiss your family anymore,
not even on the cheek.
The last time someone took your face in their palms,
you wanted to move into their night stand.
You wanted to curl up
with your head between your legs.
You wanted to do cartwheels down the street
and never come back.
You went back; but only twice.
He talked too much about Canada in his sleep.
You thought for a while he might just have a thing
for cold weather,
but she wasn't a country; she was a girl.
When you left, you texted him from the airport
because you're bad at goodbyes,
and what he said
made you cry your way onto the plane.
I know that it's hard to be hard,
but you're stronger for this.

Appetite Suppressant

It has been weeks since I've caught
even a whiff of you.

I've got the aftertaste
of someone else's mouth in my throat
because I am sick of waking up
with some part of me
growling.

I am an indiscriminate kisser.
Like a dog all shaken up
when its owner's out of town,
I am happy to see just about anyone.

Strangers all stuck up in my teeth
because I'm heart-hungry.

I Don't Know What Any of This Means

My father was the kind of man who would always pull over at the site of an accident to offer help even if phone calls had already been made, even if people were already there. It was his sole redeeming quality; he ran away only from the messes *he* made. Running into someone else's burning building was no problem— metaphorically, anyway. He never did pass his entrance interview.

My brother talks about car accidents the same way I talk about family. I don't know when he learned to forgive. I don't remember teaching him that. I don't remember learning it myself. His life's ambition is to be the man my father never was: to step up to the plate, to grow into a firefighter's uniform or ride shotgun in an ambulance.

I am still stuck on the bathroom floor with my resentment.

I lived with a man once who was so afraid of losing me that he stopped kissing me. I think he was trying to get used to the taste of my absence. I think he smelled smoke on my skin. We burnt out and I never looked back. I have grown into this cruel thing with running shoes, comfortable only when I lock myself away.

And now you.

I know that I am lucky to be alive at the same time as you. I know that finding you was a cosmic needle in a haystack, a joke of Internet cables and telephone wires. But I also know that you are more afraid of opening up than losing me. And I know that you stop at car accidents just like my father.

Today I Accidentally Told Someone That I Love You

It slipped out a little too easily, dangled off my lips,
tumbled across the bed. It was a somersaulting,
taunting affair.

I know it's not the kind of thing I should be
telling someone else. I should be whispering it into
the bends of your knees and spelling it out
with my mouth on your mouth;

but you are still too far away
and I am not braver than distance.

I am as reliable as public transportation.
I have hands made of guardrails and a train station heart;
it is full of strangers always trying to get somewhere else.
It's not a final destination.

I don't ever want to hold you back
from where you're trying to get to.

I'm sorry I never tell you what I really mean.

Improper Emergency Procedure

You have more fucking fault lines than California,
but I'd still settle somewhere along your coast
if you'd take the time to stop shifting for a moment.
I'm not afraid of the ground moving under my feet,
but I'm a little worried about your tectonic plates
grinding up against mine in a way
that sends people running for door frames.

Fresh Mint

I have written twenty-seven poems
about how it feels to be sad and still love you
at the same time
and no, baby—no—I don't mean
got up on the wrong side of the bed sad;
I mean can't get out of the bed sad.

I mean waking up with a pit in my stomach
that didn't come from a cherry.
It's nothing like a peach.
If you plant it in the ground, nothing
will grow from it.
Nothing ever grows here.

I have lips laced with guilt when you kiss me.
I watch movies about kids with cancer
and I relate when they try to push people away
because they know they're on the way down.
I always feel like I'm on the way down.

I taste like salt.
You taste like toothpaste.
There's no poetry in that. It's just life.

I Just Can't Do This Right Now

Tonight I wish I had someone's body
pressed up against mine. I am glad you are
not here to see this.

I need a man who does not look at me
the way you look at me. I need a man who is
willing to walk away from the mess in the morning.

Not like you with your telephone hands.

You are always feeling me out; you are always
calling me back. I am ringing around the wire for
you. Sometimes I forget how to want you and myself
at the same time.

I Don't Know If I'm Cut Out for This

The way you say my name makes me want to cry into
dirty pillowcases. The way you say my name makes
me want to kiss you on the mouth.

The way you say my name makes me think of
jogging down the street with a ponytail bouncing
against the back of my neck: steady, rhythmic.
Heartbeat. Pulsing. Sweat.

The way you say my name makes me believe in
caffeinated beverages: pressing palms together at the
kitchen table. Forget the church. Take me to bed instead.
Neither of us is getting any sleep.

The way you say my name reminds me of stepping
off a plane. The way you say my name reminds me of
elbow- and kneepads. The way you say my name
makes me want to try harder.

Salt

I want you to know that it is okay not to love me.
I want you to know that you are not the first person
who found it a little too tough, who took two steps
back when my jaws started snapping.

I want you to know that I look like I taste of
cigarette smoke and scotch, but I just taste like salt.
I swear that you're not missing anything but
band-aids and promises bent out of shape if you run
the wrong way when I hold out my hands.

ROLL OVER

Water Me Until I Drown

I've finally figured it out, okay? I know it took a long
time. I know it took too long.

But I don't want to be the sad girl you fuck when
you're trying to love yourself. I want to be
the house you bring potted plants into even though
you can never remember to take care of them.
I want to be the trees that remind you of home;
I want you to look at my legs and think of climbing
and broken bones and childhood games that always
left you stranded. I want you to know that I might
leave you stranded. I want you to know that you
are the only thing that slows my city down.

Promises That Don't Sound Like Promises

Sometimes you talk like I am someone's favorite coffee mug
(something familiar to keep coming back to)

and you are a single-use picnic plate,
(something flimsy and disposable).

This is me telling you that I think you are wrong.
I think we might just be pieces of the same china pattern:

breakable

breakable

but something you try to keep together.

And anyway, there's nothing wrong
with paper plate dinner dates.

I could lounge on a living room floor
and eat straight off of you
without a single damn complaint.

That's It. That's All.

I don't know how to say it,
so I'm writing it down.

I want to kiss your bad days
on the forehead.

I want to stroke your hair
in the morning.

I want to know
what your mouth tastes like
when you get off the phone
with your mother.

Like Small Children, Like Stray Dogs

I said it before (though perhaps with less grace)
and I'll say it again:

I want to take the messy parts of you in
like small children, like stray dogs.
Kiss them on the mouth, give them a place to stay.

I can't believe there are bits of you, at your age,
that are still too young to know
that they are worth taking care of.

If you don't want to look in the mirror, that's fine.
We will cover every piece of glass in the house.
We will drape sheets across the bathroom walls
and drink only out of coffee mugs;

but I am still going to marvel
at the blessing of your face
at my kitchen table.

Bunk Beds

I want to make love to you
in my childhood home,

bring your hips to my hips
in every place I ever felt small,

find better reasons
for staying up nights.

Laugh Lines

I am always moving toward you.

On my bad days, I say to myself: "then you."
Sure, this now. But then you.

I will keep tossing myself life lines.
I will keep writing myself afloat
until I don't have to write a poem
for every mile marker
from here to California.

You and I together is the most foolish thing
I've ever hoped for. You and I apart is more foolish.

When I can't sleep at night, I dream up
conversations with you. I never call. I never push.
I try not to whine. I just write it all down.

Sometimes I want to apologize
for wanting you out loud,
like too many people know the reasons
I am going to have laugh lines.

Sometimes instead of distanced pillow talk,
I want to curl up with the phone
and read you poetry.

Instead, we just talk about it.

You say, "Honey, how was your day?"
And I say, "Today I wrote another poem
about your coffee cup mouth
and all the ways you still keep me up at night."

I hear a sigh in your smile.
You make a sound that reminds me of
fighting with my bags at the airport;
but you're still too far away.

You Are My Moving Forward

How many people have told you that you feel like
coming home? I'm sure you've been somebody's shelter,
somebody's summertime, somebody's everything before
you were anything to me.

You don't remind me of home. You don't remind me
of honeysuckles or fried green tomatoes or twisted ankles.
You don't remind me of running back toward anything.

You are not safe walls to hide behind.
You are everything on the other side.

Between Your Anxieties and My Pen

I don't know how we get anything done.

You drum your fingers on my throat and think of rain on the roof of the house you grew in (not up, but sideways): the place where your last love left you alone; the place where you learned how to cope with silence and water your own plants.

And then you tell me about it—

and honey, I love to hear you talk, but I want to get in an argument with your mouth that neither of us can win, tongues twisted up like roots. I want to kiss you and feel like I am growing (and then I want to write about it).

I want to get my hair caught in the thick of you. I want you to understand that I will not always be sprouting next to you, so maybe we should take advantage of this little plot of land while we have it.

So you kiss me.

You kiss me and tell me that I taste like sand. You tell me that you have dreams of the ocean dragging me away. You tell me that you wake up afraid of riptides and ocean currents; and then you kiss me again.

And I keep thinking about waves breaking on a shore somewhere until I break away to catch some breath so I can say, "Lover, that was a pretty good line; do you mind?"

And, baby, maybe it's my fault. Maybe when I put down this pen, I'll stop looking for ways to write you in and you'll stop worrying that every word you say is filed away somewhere in writing.

Until then, maybe we'll just have to try harder to stay in the moment. Kiss me until we stop thinking about growing and ocean currents.

Kiss me until nobody cares about the metaphors anymore.

Teach Yourself to Recognize Risk but Still Take It

The first time you hear something like love
in the soft tone of his voice, do not act like he has
given you the moon.

Act like he has given you smooth blown glass,
fine china teacups: something beautiful
but absolutely breakable. Something with the potential
to be so, so sharp.

But swallow the lump in your throat.
Do not bother padding the floor. Waste no time
with an overly heavy grip. We lose so much
for fear of letting go.

You have to let it breathe. Put it to use.
It's no good tucked safely away. Roll over in the bed
and bare your neck to teeth. Just buy some thick soles
for when the glass breaks.

Please Don't Bring This Up on the Phone

I keep rewriting this poem.
I want it to make more sense.
I want it to be less honest.

I keep counting off things to blame it on.

Something about a rocky mountain high.
Something about the altitude messing with my head.
Something about missing the sound of your voice

more than anything.

I miss the sound of your voice more than anything.

Six days ago, on the bottom bunk of someone else's bed,
I wrote you some words in a marbled composition book:

"I can't go another day choking back

I love you.

I feel it in my shoulders when I breathe."

Oranges

I wake up in the middle of the night
and I text you things like "why aren't you in my bed?
come eat a bowl of oranges off of me."
I don't know what this means.
I don't even know what I'm trying to say.

Something about you and me in bed
with sticky fingers
and wet mouths
is appealing to me even in half-sleep.

Maybe oranges are a metaphor for life.
Maybe I still don't know how many seeds
I'm gonna find in you.
Maybe oranges are just supposed to mean summer heat
because I'm sick of all this cold, cold, cold.
Maybe it doesn't matter.

Maybe the only thing that means something
is that I am always waking up in the middle of the night
and reaching out to you.

You with those warm hands.
You with that wet mouth.

Little Matchstick Girl

Have you ever noticed how wanting
burns you up
from the inside out?

Like one moment I am whole,

but then I hear
your voice on the phone

and I swear to god
three blocks away from here
they can smell smoke.

Ask Again Later

I miss you so much it feels gross.
It feels wet. It feels nauseating.

I want to rip out my heart
and shake it like a Magic 8 Ball.
Is this okay, is this okay, is this okay,
or does it make me weak?

Coffee Cups and Fruit Poems

Five hours since I heard it last,
I miss your voice again.
There is something to be said for all of this missing
but I do not know what it is.
I just know that it feels right to say it.
I miss you.
I miss you.

Like coming down from a caffeine high,
I'm still figuring it out.

Oh, boy. Oh, man. Oh, you mess.
What right do you have to leave me like this?
Questioning all of my other love poems.
Writing odes to fruit
and thinking about the taste of you.
I miss you.

I miss you in some wild way.
Some rain smell on the earth kind of way.
Some scratching your name into trees kind of way.
Some scratching my name into you kind of way.
Even this poem is me marking my territory.
Tell me this counts for something.

To Be a Metaphor for Starlight

I write about you
like I wouldn't mind scalding my mouth on you.
I write about mountains, and stars,
and the curve of you:
some hiker's trail spine I'd like to get lost along,
some light in all this dark.

Something wild. Something I'd like to map out.
Something like an earthquake
or a bicycle wreck.
Something I need elbow- and kneepads for.

Twenty metaphors for fucking,
twenty-six for fucking distance
and I still can't blame you for not wanting to cross it,
for keeping your hands to yourself,
for reading all of these poems and not wanting
to get caught up in the mess.

Not wanting to be a peach
or a bowl of oranges spread out on the bed.
Not wanting to be a metaphor for starlight
or a bottle of Shiraz
or fir trees.

Not wanting to be a man with a coffee cup mouth.

Just wanting to be a man
alone somewhere
without all the fuss.

The Most Magnificent Pastime

He said, "I never want to pull out of you"
and I think I fell in love. What a fucked up thing to do.

And this wasn't supposed to be a fucked up poem
but it's turning into a fucked up poem
because I haven't been able to come in three years
without thinking of his hips sliding into mine: like first base,
like second base, like third base,

like home.

Before You Leave Me

The sky has that just before rain smell
and your hands are knotted in my hair.

We are people with arms intertwined
like the pattern on a tartan scarf.

We are people with arms intertwined
almost like lovers hesitant to say goodbye
(but not quite).

There is a warning in the wind whipping around us.
I smell fear on you like a dog
but I don't say

anything.

We Both Know What It Is

Watch me knock over every cup of coffee
poured in this house.
Watch me rip the pits out of fruit
just to throw the whole thing away.
I don't know how to be angry with you.

I don't know why I thought the sound of your voice
could make up for all the bad things
that ever happened to me.

I tried to write poems about your leaving
before you left me
because I was scared;
now I write them because I don't know what
else to do in your absence.

You have ripped something from both of us
but I don't know what it is.

I'm sorry I have to lie to make it easy.

Ask Me to Stay

Tell me that you have been dreaming of me.
That you wake up in cold sweats, gulping in air.
You feel like you've drowned. You wake up and
still feel like you're drowning.

Tell me that you've spent a great deal of time
gazing at stars, thinking that sometimes things look
better farther apart. That constellations are beautiful
only because we have the space to connect the dots.

Now take it back. Tell me that you're sorry. That you
know we're not stars. We're just people. Tell me that
you know there's nothing poetic about plane tickets.
Tell me that you want to buy them anyway.

Ask me to stay.

I Swear Somewhere This Works

In a parallel universe or another world
or a different life,

we sit across from each other

at the kitchen table

and go over
the grocery
list.

I Forgive You for Not Meeting Me on the Bridge

You have EXIT sign lips.
Something I want to run toward in case
of emergency.

And everything is an emergency.
Lover, I'm out of bread and milk,
come lay your hands on me.

I'm writing another love poem because
I don't know how to write about The Bad Stuff yet.
The Crying and The Leaving. The Giving Up. The
way I want to beat my fists against walls and break
every plate in my house. The way I want to shove
words back into my mouth and learn to swallow
everything whole.

Tell me that you feel it, too. Tell me that you have
flooded like the Amazon in monsoon season.
Everything you love is wet.

Everything I love is lost somewhere downstream.

You have seen me through all of my dog days. I want
to repay you with mouth to mouth. With coffee in bed.
With nights spent next to you. I want to repay you by
stealing all of your blankets and wearing your shirts
and keeping the AC on all winter just so I have an
excuse to stay close.

Before I met you, I never would have let anything
get this far.

That is the "love" in this love poem. I took your hand
and wanted to walk out onto something unsteady. I
wanted to take the leap. The jump. The fall from a very
tall building. I wanted the mess of it. All of it.

I wanted you in your slippers with the dog
you've had for eight months and still haven't named.
I wanted you. You and your Californian fault lines.
You and that coffee cup mouth. You and those hands
made for cradling fruit and steering wheels and the
phone and me.

I don't know how to do this.

Me.

I don't know how to walk away from you.

Maybe that is the blessing in all of this mess.
Maybe if you came into my life to teach me one thing,
it was to hang up my running shoes for a while.
Not just to want to.

I keep thinking of when we met. Long-distance
phone calls. Those nights you used to lay on
your bedroom floor in the dark and I would muffle
my voice with pillows and blankets, hunkered down
in my own bed. We would talk until the sun was up here,
but three thousand miles away, you were still
a little behind me.

I guess it's still like that. You are far enough behind
to love me but not be able to say it. And I have been
far enough ahead to see the end of this. Baby, it doesn't
look very good. Baby, at some point it just stopped
making sense.

I don't know how to be angry with you, but my pride
demands I figure it out. It is so easy to make monsters
out of the people I have loved, to pick up a pen and
write "THIS IS YOUR FAULT" until the page is full.
It is easier to make myself the monster, to snap and bite

and run and hide. It is easy to bare my teeth.

It is harder to be honest.

Nobody here has claws or sharp teeth.

I am not the bomb and I am not the city where
it went off: buildings crumbled, everything ash.
The casualties are not my fault, but the aftermath
is a mess.

Sometimes things don't work.

And that's it.

We ran around the wire. A tin can telephone
stretched as far as it could go without breaking.

And then it broke.

Acknowledgements

This little book has received a lot of help and the only reason it's come to fruition is because a couple of other people have offered up their love and support consistently during the process of writing all of this and then stitching it together into something coherent. Affection and absolute gratitude to:

Caitlyn Siehl for the late night text messages and for reading this mess before anyone else; Fortesa Latifi for checking in on me; Emily Keenan for just existing in the world; Rachel Drummond for knowing the whole story; Krystle Alder for putting up with all of my vague design requests and still coming through with something lovely; Clementine von Radics and WAYP for giving this book its first home—

& you, for reading, always.

About The Author

Trista Mateer is a writer and poet living outside of Baltimore, Maryland. She believes in lipstick, black tea, and owning more books than she can ever possibly read. The author of two collections of poetry, she is also known for her eponymous blog.

To find out more, write or visit her on Twitter @tristamateer or at tristamateer@gmail.com.

See more work at: **tristamateer.com**.

CPSIA information can be obtained at www.ICGtesting.com
Printed in the USA
LVOW10s1555090216

474362LV00024B/1235/P